AGILE

SOFTWARE

DEVELOPMENT

AGILE, SCRUM, AND

KANBAN, FOR

PROJECT

MANAGEMENT

Peter Oliver

AGILE SOFTWARE DEVELOPMENT

Copyright © 2018 by Concise Reads™

TABLE OF CONTENTS

INTRODUCTION

Agile is a software development management framework developed to streamline the development process and focus on rapid delivery. While no official list exists of companies that use Agile, IBM is known to openly use this method to develop software.

Traditionally, software development was completed in cycles of six to eighteen months. If we go all the way back to the 1990s, development cycles could take up to three years. The problem with this timeline is that business needs moved at a much faster pace. The needs of the company were likely to change before development finished creating a need for better and more streamlined software development processes.

One improvement made was breaking the development cycle into small deliverable chunks, but then a new problem arose.

When we begin to connect the smaller chunks of development together, we found they were not compatible with each other, and we had to make numerous changes and often rethink the solution. This also took considerable time and effort.

It wasn't until 2001 when seventeen software developers met at the Snowbird resort in Utah and put together a document known as 'The Manifesto for Agile Software Development' that incorporated all the lightweight software development methods of the 1990s, such as Scrum (1995), into a working draft of best practices.

This document was modified over many years until the creation of the 'Agile Glossary' in 2011—an open source repository of knowledge by the world's agile practitioners.

The original manifesto begins with its four values for starting an Agile project:

> "We are uncovering better ways of developing software by doing it and helping others do it. Through this work we have come to value:"

1. Individuals and interactions over processes and tools

2. Working software over comprehensive documentation

3. Customer collaboration over contract negotiation

4. Responding to change over following a plan

"That is, while there is value in the items on the right, we value the items on the left more."

In this Concise Reads guide, we'll walk you through the basics of Agile and Agile methods such as Scrum and Kanban, so you could use this framework in the management of your next software development project. At its simplest form, think of the framework as a way to reduce inefficiency through rapid prototyping, cross-functional team set up, and clearly defined non-overlapping roles. The proven assumption was that by iterating through the entire development cycle multiple times, a learning curve begins to take effect that produces efficiency gains.

CYNEFIN FRAMEWORK

There are many management frameworks, and there is no way to cover them all in an hour, but I'd like you to understand where the most common ones fit, and where Agile is best utilized. To do this we use a conceptual framework developed by IBM called Cynefin, which is a Welsh word meaning habitat, and used here as understanding your 'sense of place' with regards to different management situations.

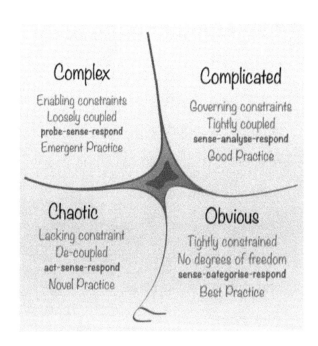

First, break up the world of projects into four categories:

1. **Complex (unknown, unknowns):** Cause and effect can only be linked in retrospect. In this situation, the manager is recommended to **probe-sense-respond**. If the cost of failing is low, then it is better to constantly probe rather than to act. This is the situation for early stage software development, and this is the best use case for the Agile framework.

2. **Complicated (known, unknowns):** In this situation, we know there are unknowns, and the only way to connect cause and effect is through methodical expert analysis. This is the situation faced by professionals such as doctors, lawyers, and other experts. The guideline is to **sense-analyze-respond** and use the LEAN framework.

3. **Obvious (known-knowns):** These are known problems with known best practices, and the guideline is to **sense-categorize-respond** (with best practices). For example, when you find the product error rate is high, then you would use LEAN SIX SIGMA which has been shown to reduce errors of the final output.

4. **Chaotic:** In this situation, cause and effect is not clear, and the manager's role is to stem the bleeding by acting first. The guideline is to **act-sense-respond**. An example of this is the 9/11 attacks, where firefighters did not know what caused the incident to happen, and instead acted first to stem the chaos, and then analyzed all the facts.

5. **Disorder:** This is a situation that likely applies to the other four, but the manager does not know where to place it. It fills the void among the four domains. In this instance, the guideline is to break up the situation, so that its components fit within the other four and the manager can act accordingly.

The manager can move different parts of the project among the four domains.

For example, if a <u>chaotic</u> situation is under control, then the manager can move to the complex domain and begin probing to find the problem. If a <u>complex</u> problem is now understood, then we move out of Agile and spend expert resources to deconstruct the problem and answer the cause and effect. If the cause and effect are known and there are best practices to dictate development, then the manager moves from <u>complicated</u> to the <u>obvious</u> domain.

Therefore, when first creating a new product, a manager would start with AGILE. After the product is completed, and we begin to make it market ready, then the manager would use LEAN. Finally, for a commercial ready product, the focus is on operations, and the manager would employ LEAN SIX SIGMA.

VALUE CHAIN:

AGILE→LEAN→LEAN SIX SIGMA

This guide will cover Agile software development. The next guide in the series will cover both Lean and Lean Six Sigma.

PRINCIPLES OF AGILE

The biggest value of the twelve principles of Agile software development comes from the first three principles. I want you to keep in mind three words: **Value**, **Quality**, and **Flow**.

Making sure each step delivers value will help you meet your deadline. Making sure each step produces the intended quality will lead to a project within scope. Controlling the flow of work means reducing total development costs. So again, keep **Value**, **Quality**, and **Flow** in mind.

For completeness, the original twelve principles from the Manifesto of Agile Software Development are:

1. Our highest priority is to <u>satisfy the customer</u> through early and continuous delivery of valuable software.

2. Welcome changing requirements, even late in development. Agile processes <u>harness change</u> for the customer's competitive advantage.

3. Deliver <u>working software frequently</u>, from a couple of weeks to a couple of months, with a preference to the shorter timescale.

4. Business people and developers must <u>work together daily</u> throughout the project.

5. Build projects around motivated individuals. Give them the <u>environment and support</u> they need and trust them to get the job done.

6. The most efficient and effective method of conveying information to and within a

development team is <u>face-to-face conversation</u>.

7. <u>Working software</u> is the primary measure of progress.

8. Agile processes promote sustainable development. The sponsors, developers, and users should be able to maintain a <u>constant pace indefinitely</u>.

9. Continuous attention to <u>technical excellence and good design</u> enhances agility.

10. <u>Simplicity</u>--the art of maximizing the amount of work not done--is essential.

11. The best architectures, requirements, and designs emerge from <u>self-organizing teams</u>.

12. At regular intervals, <u>the team reflects</u> on how to become more effective, then tunes and adjusts its behavior accordingly.

PRINCIPLE #1: DELIVER VALUE EARLY AND OFTEN

Before embarking on Agile project, the manager with the team's input needs to write the **must**-haves or needs, **should**-haves, and **could**-haves or as others call it 'nice-to-have'. Remember, the customer is happiest when their most important needs are met faster and more often rather than waiting for the feature-packed release two years away.

There are several ways of defining this feature set. The overarching industry term is to use '**design thinking**' which consists of 1. User story maps, 2. Business model canvas, 3. Impact mapping. All three are linked with the same concept which is—know thy customer.

One tried and true method is to create personas of the end customer and detail what their most basic immediate needs are, and break those up into **must** haves to build a working proto-type, and **should**-haves to appeal to the end customer. Lastly, pepper in the **could**-haves or nice-to-haves that are not necessarily required to satisfy the customer but that may make the product more appealing. Once you've clearly identified the **must**, **should**, and **could** haves, then focus only on the must haves for your first agile iteration to deliver the maximum value. Other considerations to take into account when developing this list are:

- Change in profit
- Change in resources required (this could be technical or business resources)

- Deadlines
- External requirements (for example minimum regulatory requirements)

PRINCIPLE #2: OPTIMIZE FLOW

This is very important to reduce cost, and to be able to adapt to changing feature requirements. We touched on this subject in the Operations Management Concise Reads.

As a reminder:

Flow = Lead Time + WIP (work in progress)

Flow Efficiency = WIP/Lead Time

Lead time is how long it takes for production from start to finish and how long it takes for delivery to the customer. WIP (work in progress) is how long each productive step takes. WIP time is interchangeable with cycle time (CT) which is used in Lean production. Therefore, to reduce costs and maximize flow efficiency, we need to maximize WIP relative to lead time. Keep in mind lead time also includes the time between moving from one station's WIP to the next (also known as 'waiting' in Lean production).

Effective methods to maximize flow efficiency are:

1) Reduce batch size
2) Limit WIP (example: reduce inventory)
3) Remove system constraints
4) Remove waste

In software development, we reduce batch sizes by reducing the deliverables into manageable chunks so there is no buildup of inventory along the development cycle.

We limit WIP by breaking up chunks into multiple steps and avoiding **context switching**, so each developer is doing the same type of job using the same tools.

We co-locate cross functional teams to remove system constraints and hence lead time.

We remove waste by decreasing inventory, and following a system of pull not push production (which leads to overproduce and hence waste). This involves putting completed tasks in a queue where the next developer pulls from when they are ready. If we inundated the next developer in the sequence with push requests, their WIP cycle team decreases. This is the concept behind Kanban.

PRINCIPLE #3: QUALITY THROUGH FAST FEEDBACK

The two aspects of ensuring quality and thus meeting our deadline is to VALIDATE and VERIFY quickly.

The faster the feedback, the lower the overall cost and the faster we meet deadlines. Feedback for **validation** relates to whether we are building the <u>right</u> product, and feedback for **verification** relates to whether we are building it <u>correctly</u>.

In software development early feedback comes from the following:

1. Pair programming
   a. Two developers work on the same workstation, one is the driver, and the other is the reviewer. This requires more resources but has been shown to reduce errors by at least 15% and is useful in the probing phase of Agile software development.

2. Continuous integration

    a. Developers post their code changes to the same repository as other developers and do so often to catch any integration conflicts or failures early on.

3. Test Driven Development (TDD)

    a. At its core it simply involves creating a test that the code must pass before being committed to the repository of code.

4. Active Stakeholder Participation

    a. This allows the user stories to be changed early if needed through active stakeholder participation. This is the job of the Product Owner in Scrum, and we'll cover that later in this guide.

5. Model Storming

a. This encourages a developer who hit a bottleneck to grab a few teammates to help him or her solve the problem before continuing back on their tasks. In Scrum, the product owner and tech lead would be the ones involved to ensure the other developers are not distracted.

6. Parallel Testing

a. This involves testing the new code while the old code is still running. Once the new code has proved it is working, the developers then jump onto the new code repository; this again is used to limit start/stops when adding new code.

Fast feedback using these methods and others allows for small continuous improvements in the flow process, and ultimately increases our flow efficiency with each improvement.

SCRUM

The three foundations of scrum are

1. **Transparency:** relates to roles and tasks
2. **Inspection:** relates to the structured meetings
3. **Adaptation:** relates the feedback and iterative process

Originally, development followed the waterfall process of **plan, build, test, and review**. Sprint is literally a sprint through plan, build, test, and review in 1-2 weeks to produce an almost shippable product and then repeated multiple times over the development cycle. The purpose of running through all phases of development quickly is to build experience in what works and what doesn't so the next iteration has improved value, quality, and flow.

The 3 roles of SCRUM:

1. **Scrum Master**: This is the team organizer and facilitator. They are like a professional rugby coach empowered to keep their players following agile practices, protecting them from disturbances, and coordinating the Agile inspect and adapt meetings.

   A great video of a Scum Master's duties can be found below. Note the commentator is Jeff Sutherland, one of the original contributors of the *Manifesto for Software Agile Development*.

   https://youtu.be/P6v-I9VvTq4

2. **Product Owner**: This is the person in charge of defining the requirements of the product, supports their team to deliver on time and in-scope, and is the one who ultimately decides if the user story has met acceptance criteria. The PO literally owns the product backlog, prioritizes the items in the backlog based on feedback, and creates the acceptance criteria for the backlog items. The product backlog is a document, typically an excel sheet with all the user stories that will eventually be developed. Prioritization of the user stories allows the PO to decide what will be developed in each week's sprint. Acceptance criteria (including unit testing criteria)for completed user stories can be created using a domain specific language in a process known as Behavior-Driven-

Development or BDD. To make it as logical as possible for developers, the PO would write out the acceptance criteria in logical syntax, whether through a program language or in English using logical modifiers like Boolean algebra (AND, OR, NOT).

3. **Cross Functional Team**: The team is typically no larger than 5 to 9 individuals, with the product owner and scrum master occupying two managerial positions, and the remaining positions are for 3-4 developers, potentially an inspector/tester, and technical lead who sets the agenda.

In Scrum, a **user story** is created that defines the user role (customer), functionality, and business value. The typical template is "As a <type of user>, I want <a feature>, so that <some value is created>". A simple example for a health insurance user story could be "As a member, I would like to find out my remaining plan benefits, which will drive preventative behavior and lower overall long-term cost to the insurer."

The **user story** is then broken down into development **tasks**. The team calculates its **capacity** in the form of points, with 1 point = 8 hours (this can be changed), and then each task is assigned capacity points. This way, only the most important tasks are assigned capacity points and there is a clear guideline on the lead time for the user story to be completed.

Typical scrum cycles can range from 1-4 weeks with the product owner acting as the owner of the user story, able to answer questions for the developers. The capacity is divided in such a way that the entire software development process is accounted for including planning, requirements analysis, design, coding, testing, and review.

SCRUM CEREMONIES

There are three processes and five meetings that keep the pace. The processes are very important for the product manager and can be set up using a number of software packages, with the most basic of them being a simple excel sheet.

These are:

1. **Product Backlog**: product features are prioritized, and their value to the business is defined. This is a sheet with all the needs, shoulds, and could haves along with values assigned to them for prioritization based on other considerations like costs or potential profit generation.

2. **Sprint Backlog**: team capacity is
   <u>assigned</u> for user stories, and deadlines
   are assigned for the different tasks for
   this week's sprint.

3. **Scrum Board**: this is similar to the
   Kanban board, but while the Kanban is
   more general purpose for pull requests, a
   scrum board provides transparency on
   what stage of the plan, build, test, and
   review software development cycle the
   team is in. Here is a fun scene from
   Silicon Valley, the television show,
   showing a Scrum board

   https://youtu.be/oyVksFviJVE

Meetings are another set of agile ceremonies
that manage shorter feedback loops. There are
5 meetings in Agile, and these are:

1. **Spring Planning**: Review the product backlog and write out the sprint backlog. Get buy-in from the team on expectations (sprint metrics) and deadlines.

2. **Daily StandUp**: These are quick 15 minute meetings that answer three questions in order to update the scrum board with progress and obstacles the PO needs to address. The three questions are:
   a. What did I accomplish yesterday?
   b. What do I plan to accomplish today?
   c. What obstacles do I foresee?

3. **Sprint Review**: After the sprint, the product is reviewed, and key metrics are

calculated and shared with the team. If the goal of the product sprint was to cut down on number of user clicks for example, then a simple key metric must be # of user clicks. Additionally, new user stories are added, or old ones are updated for the next sprint.

4. **Sprint Retrospective:** After each sprint, the processes are evaluated by the team with the purpose to improve the flow process for the next sprint. This includes all processes such as hand-offs, resource utilization, or communication.

5. **Backlog Refinement**: This is a constant process. The backlog needs to be edited to reflect new information with regards to feature requirements. The PO is in charge of this master document based on

testing, feedback, and active stakeholder participation.

KANBAN

Kanban originated in lean manufacturing but found wide spread adoption in software development. It is a visual process management tool that allows <u>pulled work</u> as capacity permits rather than pushed work that leads to overproduction and waste. It can be applied for any development process and its purpose is to limit WIP while allowing flexibility in resource management. Often we hear of Scrumban, which is the natural evolution of extending Scrum to Kanban. While Scrum is firmly rooted in cycles of sprints that go through all phases of product development, namely plan, build, test, and review, Kanban is the visual representation of smaller tasks within each phase of product development. You can think of Kanban as a blowout of the scrum board.

Kanban is based on six principles:

1. **Visualization**: this involves agreeing with your team on the steps in a WIP such as sources identified, design mockup, low fidelity prototype, build, test, and requirements for being marked 'done'.

2. **Limiting work in progress (typical agile)**: prevent context switching, reduce waste, and force prioritization are key elements. This differs depending on the task being completed and is best managed by understanding capacity requirements for each WIP.

3. **Flow management (typical agile)**: not every WIP is equal, that is why it is important to devote appropriate capacity

to the different WIP such as placing two points on development and 1 point on testing for example. Part of flow management means reassessing if these initial point allocations make sense and readjusting as needed.

4. **Making policies explicit**: clearly define what 'done' means. In Scrum, this is the product owner's job and in Kanban it allows clear and explicit understanding of when a post-it or board can be moved from one station to the next without having a third party like a product owner.

5. **Using feedback loops (typical agile)**: The Japanese word 'Kaizen' means 'change for better' and used in the context of small changes for **continuous improvement**. Feedback whether daily

or weekly is meant to define what is not working and how it can be improved. In Kanban, this feedback loop is known by the acronym of PDCA or plan-do-check-act. In Scrum, we call this the inspect-adapt principle.

6. **Collaborative or experimental evolution (typical agile)**: this is also typical of agile philosophy in a complex situation where fast probing is encouraged. In Scrum, these are known as technical spikes where a problem needs to be probed further before being scoped in the sprint backlog. In Kanban, this means being flexible to change requirements, resource allocation, and policies based on new information.

The process starts with a Kanban board.

Originally in the form of post-its on a physical board, today a Kanban board is created using software like Trello or Jira.

In large fortune 500 companies, a 'ticket' is issued when there is a tech problem, and the technical lead or product owner would assign the ticket to a developer using a digital Kanban board. This provides transparency to the manager but also to the employee that issued the ticket to see where in the process the issue is managed, whether in queue, in progress, or done.

Communication between the issuer of the ticket and the developer or technician assigned to the task is limited through the Kanban board so that interruptions are minimized.

CONCLUSION

This quick 1-hour guide was meant to introduce you to the Agile principles, the components of Scrum, and the more lightweight Kanban framework for project management. For a deeper dive into these principles, one can obtain the Agile Certified Practitioner (ACP) from the Project Management Institute (PMI). The Scrum Alliance offers 6 different certifications (https://www.scrumalliance.org/certifications). These are costly, but valuable if you are planning a career in project management.

Additionally, for project managers leading very large enterprise development cycles, certification in Scaled Agile For lean Enterprise or **SAFe** certification is valuable.

For startups, small enterprises, general managers, and non-managing roles, this Concise Reads is enough to get you started. Gaining experience is of utmost importance, and even participating in an ad-hoc sprint will lend a deeper appreciation of the flexibility and rapid cycle of Agile development.

Just remember that your **product backlog** is the most important document to begin with. If you hire an external development team, whether for backend or frontend work, the first call is typically to create personas in order to fill the product backlog. You will be asked as a product owner to identify the end customer, their background, their needs, and what solution would solve those needs. These solutions are then placed in the product backlog and broken down into tasks when you get to the sprint planning phase.

The outcome is the same, that is to fill the product backlog by knowing thy customer. The approach to identify **must haves** might differ slightly whether using personas, filling out a business model canvas clearly identifying all stakeholders and their needs, or building out a customer journey to identify their needs and seeing where your solution would fit along that customer journey. Please understand that it is all a starting point to draft the product backlog which is not static but rather dynamic and will be changed when new information becomes available. Think of the product backlog as the business plan for your software development project. Therefore, identify the customer pain points using any approach you like and start phrasing those needs into user stories to add to the product backlog.

Also worthwhile is to give a digital Kanban service a try. Try the free version of Trello to get a sense of setting boards and columns.

Good luck, and feel free to share your copy or purchase additional copies for your team if they are new to Scrum. Remember the goal is a working software product using the Scrum ceremonies, and with an agile focus on value, quality, and flow to maximize productivity.

Hope you enjoyed this quick guide, for any additional topics in management, be sure to send us a request by email.